Should All Children Get VACCINES?

By Naomi Osborne

KidHaven
PUBLISHING

Published in 2020 by
KidHaven Publishing, an Imprint of Greenhaven Publishing, LLC
353 3rd Avenue
Suite 255
New York, NY 10010

Designer: Deanna Paternostro
Editor: Vanessa Oswald

Photo credits: Cover Photographee.eu/Shutterstock.com; p. 5 (top) Poprotskiy Alexey/Shutterstock.com; p. 5 (bottom) Chris Maddaloni/Roll Call/Getty Images; p. 7 Jezper/Shutterstock.com; p. 9 Creativa Images/Shutterstock.com; p. 11 Jonny Essex/Shutterstock.com; pp. 13, 15, 21 (inset, left) Monkey Business Images/Shutterstock.com; pp. 17, 21 (inset, right) Bilanol/Shutterstock.com; p. 19 bunyarit klinsukhon/Shutterstock.com; p. 21 (notepad) ESB Professional/Shutterstock.com; p. 21 (markers) Kucher Serhii/Shutterstock.com; p. 21 (photo frame) FARBAI/iStock/Thinkstock; p. 21 (inset, middle) Rawpixel.com/Shutterstock.com.

Cataloging-in-Publication Data

Names: Osborne, Naomi.
Title: Should all children get vaccines? / Naomi Osborne.
Description: New York : KidHaven Publishing, 2020. | Series: Points of view | Includes glossary and index.
Identifiers: ISBN 9781534532038 (pbk.) | ISBN 9781534531918 (library bound) | ISBN 9781534532090 (6 pack) | ISBN 9781534531970 (ebook)
Subjects: LCSH: Vaccines–Juvenile literature. | Vaccination–Juvenile literature. | Vaccination–Public opinion–Juvenile literature.
Classification: LCC RA638.O826 2020 | DDC 615.3'72–dc23

Printed in the United States of America

Some of the images in this book illustrate individuals who are models. The depictions do not imply actual situations or events.

CPSIA compliance information: Batch #BW20KL: For further information contact Greenhaven Publishing LLC, New York, New York at 1-844-317-7404.

Please visit our website, www.greenhavenpublishing.com. For a free color catalog of all our high-quality books, call toll free 1-844-317-7404 or fax 1-844-317-7405.

CONTENTS

An Ongoing
DEBATE

Every year, many children get vaccines, or shots, to **prevent** them from getting diseases, or sicknesses. In the past, these diseases weren't always preventable, but after vaccines were invented for them, now they are.

Some people think that vaccines are harmful for children to get. They believe vaccines cause other problems for a child's health. The vaccination **debate** continues as some people think it's not safe to vaccinate children, while many others think all children should get them so they can stay healthy and not spread diseases to others.

Know the Facts!

As of 2017, 70.4 percent of children between 19 months and 35 months old in the United States were vaccinated for deadly, preventable diseases, such as measles.

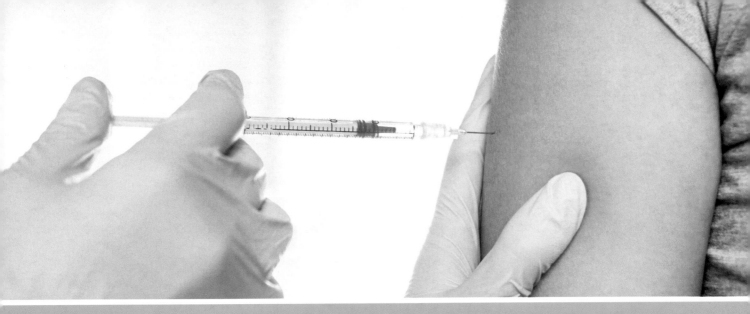

Many people believe all children should be vaccinated, but some people have a different opinion. It's important to know why people have different points of view, whether you agree with them or not.

How Vaccines
WORK

A vaccine is made up of weakened or dead germs called antigens that act like a specific disease that could enter the body. Once these germs are injected, or put, into the body, immune cells such as white blood cells, which **protect** against disease, attack these germs with **antibodies**. This helps the body remember these harmful antigens to fight off the disease if the body ever comes across it again.

Some of the most common vaccines offered to children are for chickenpox and measles. Children typically receive these vaccines before they start going to school.

Know the Facts!

Vaccines weren't always available to prevent diseases. In 1796, Edward Jenner invented the first successful vaccine, which protected people against smallpox.

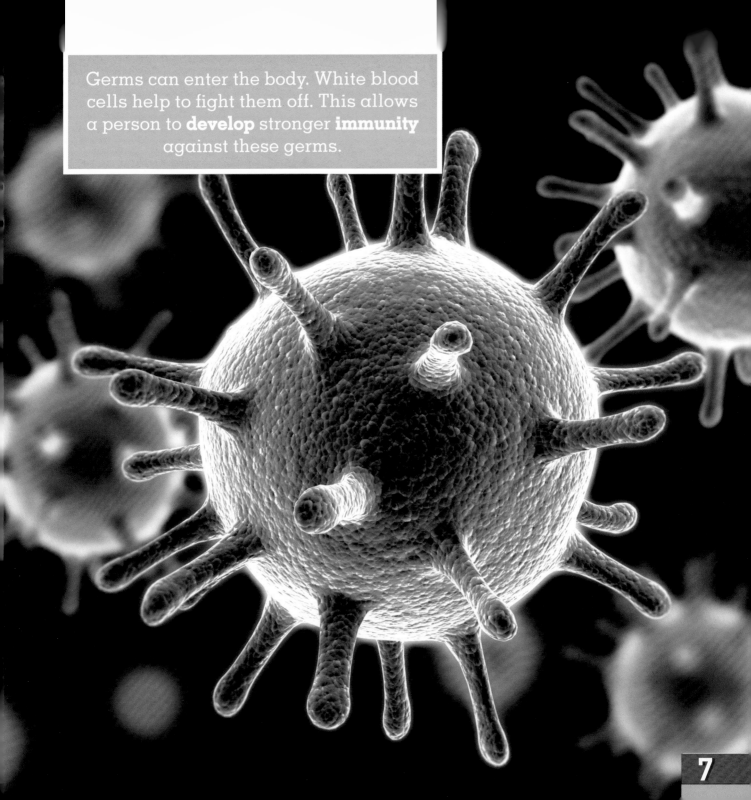

Germs can enter the body. White blood cells help to fight them off. This allows a person to **develop** stronger **immunity** against these germs.

Making the World
HEALTHIER

There are many benefits of vaccination, such as preventing diseases in children at an age when they're most at risk. Vaccines also protect against more diseases than ever before due to advances in science and medicine.

Some diseases that used to harm or kill people have been **eliminated** or almost eliminated because of vaccines. One disease that was eliminated because of vaccines in 1980 was smallpox. This disease caused a rash and other problems, such as a high fever, and it was often deadly.

Know the Facts!

Vaccines currently prevent between 2 million and 3 million deaths every year.

Scientists, doctors, and health care workers have made sure vaccines are safe before giving them to children.

Vaccines and
AUTISM

Some people are against vaccinating their children because they believe it causes other problems, such as autism spectrum disorder (ASD), which is a **developmental disorder**. Signs of autism include problems with social skills and speech. Scientists don't exactly know what the cause of autism is, so they continue to study the disorder in hopes of one day finding the cause and better treatments.

The majority of scientists, doctors, and public health **researchers** believe there's no proof that vaccines cause autism. However, some parents and guardians still believe they're protecting their children by choosing not to vaccinate them.

Know the Facts!

A 2018 report showed that 1 in 59 children are said to have autism spectrum disorder.

There are many false claims on the internet about vaccines being linked to autism, which can scare parents into believing their children are safer unvaccinated. Parents should make sure they're reading **reliable** studies and sources before making choices about their children's health.

EVERYONE

Vaccines don't just protect those who are getting them. They also stop the spread of disease from person to person, creating what's called herd immunity. This means a large population will be protected against a disease because many of them have gotten vaccinated.

If many people who are able to get vaccines get them, this helps better protect those who can't get vaccines due to health problems. It also keeps children who are too young to be vaccinated from getting many diseases. Both infants and toddlers are at a high risk of catching diseases.

Know the Facts!

Some diseases spread more easily than others. Each measles case will spread to about 16 to 18 more people. Each case of the flu will only make between 2 and 3 more people sick with the flu.

Vaccinating one child can keep many other children from getting sick too.

PROBLEMS

Not all children can get all vaccines. They may have health problems that make it impossible for them to be vaccinated for some diseases. Also, people who've had **allergic reactions** to the first dose of a vaccine are generally told not to get more doses. These people shouldn't get vaccines.

Some people don't want their children to get vaccines because of possible side effects. These include pain, swelling, and **fatigue**. However, others argue that these side effects can be unpleasant, but they're still less harmful than the diseases vaccines prevent.

Know the Facts!

Harmful side effects from vaccines are rare. Studies show if 1 million doses of a vaccine are given, 1 to 2 people may have a bad allergic reaction.

Not all parents agree with required vaccinations for children. They fear too many vaccinations early on will weaken their children's immune systems.

An Informed
OPINION

While there are people on both sides of the vaccination debate with strong opinions, the facts about vaccines are available. Most childhood vaccines are between 90 and 99 percent effective in preventing disease.

Even when vaccines don't completely prevent diseases, they can still help the people who get them. If for some reason a child still got sick with a disease after getting a vaccine for it, the disease would generally be less harmful than if the child hadn't gotten the vaccine.

Know the Facts!

In 2019, a measles outbreak in New York State brought the number of measles cases up to more than 900. That was the highest level in the United States since the disease was thought to have been eliminated in 2000.

Diseases such as measles are easily preventable if parents get their children vaccinated before they're **exposed** to the germs that cause them. However, measles cases have been on the rise as more parents choose not to vaccinate their children.

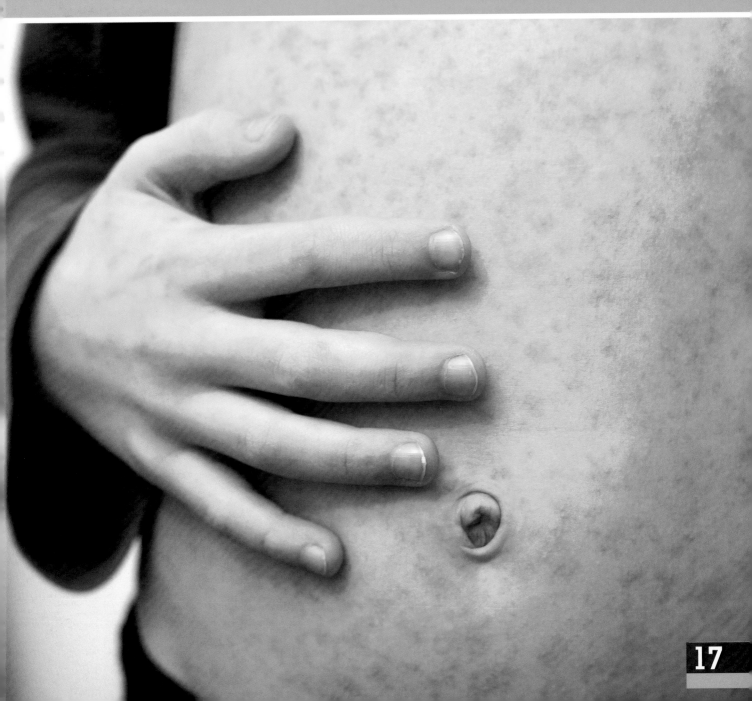

The Freedom to
CHOOSE

Some people don't believe the government should have a say in their personal medical choices, which includes whether or not to vaccinate their children. They believe they should have the freedom to choose the kind of health care they give their children and don't believe vaccines should be required.

Other people don't vaccinate their children because of religious reasons. A person's religion is the belief system they choose to follow, and it plays a part in how they live their lives. People have the right to religious freedom, which means they can refuse to do things because of their religious beliefs.

Know the Facts!

Two major religions in the United States that **discourage** vaccination are the Church of Christ, Scientist, whose followers are called Christian Scientists, and the Dutch Reformed Church.

It's important to respect a person's right to freedom of religion.

Choosing Your Own
POINT OF VIEW

It's important when choosing your own point of view on any topic to consider both sides of the argument. Many people feel strongly about vaccinating their children in order to prevent them from getting diseases. People on the other side of this debate feel vaccinations are unsafe for their children for multiple reasons and want to protect them by not having them vaccinated.

People on both sides of this debate believe they're making the right choice for their children. However, children can have their own point of view too. What do you think? Should all children get vaccines?

Know the Facts!

Famous people who've openly supported vaccines include Jennifer Garner, Jon Stewart, Julie Bowen, Kristen Bell, Salma Hayek, and Sarah Michelle Gellar.

Should all children get vaccines?

YES

- Vaccinating children protects them against diseases and boosts their immune system.

- A person who gets a vaccine but still gets sick will generally not get as sick as they would have without the vaccine.

- Vaccines create herd immunity.

- Vaccines are almost 100-percent effective at preventing the spread of many diseases.

NO

- Giving children too many vaccines all at once may weaken their immune system.

- Some sources claim that vaccines can cause developmental disorders or have harmful side effects.

- Not all children can get certain vaccines because of allergies or other health problems.

- People should have the freedom to choose how they protect their children from diseases.

Making a chart of reasons why people support or don't support a practice, such as vaccinating children, can help people clearly see both points of view before making an informed decision about an issue.

21

GLOSSARY

allergic reaction: A health problem that happens after coming in contact with something the body thinks is harmful but is not.

antibody: A substance made by special cells that helps fight off germs and diseases in the body.

debate: An argument or discussion about an issue, generally between two sides.

develop: To build, change, or create over time.

developmental disorder: A mental health problem a child has early in life having to do with language, communication, social skills, and motor skills.

discourage: To get someone not to do something.

eliminate: To get rid of something.

expose: To come in contact with something.

fatigue: A feeling of being tired.

immunity: The body's ability to fight off infections and diseases.

prevent: To stop something from happening.

protect: To keep safe.

reliable: Able to be trusted.

researcher: A person who studies something very closely.

For More
INFORMATION

WEBSITES

BrainPop: Vaccines

www.brainpop.com/health/diseasesinjuriesandconditions/vaccines/
This website includes activites and games for children that make learning about vaccines fun.

KidsHealth: Your Child's Immunizations

kidshealth.org/en/parents/vaccine.html
KidsHealth is one of the most trusted sources for information and advice on children's health. This website provides information on the different types of vaccines, what diseases they prevent, and an explanation of how vaccines work.

BOOKS

Brundle, Joanna. *Vaccines.* King's Lynn, England: BookLife, 2019.

Havemeyer, Janie. *Smallpox: How a Pox Changed History.* North Mankato, MN: Capstone Press, 2019.

Senker, Cath. *The Science of Medical Technology, Vaccines, and Health Care.* Brighton, England: Book House, 2019.

INDEX